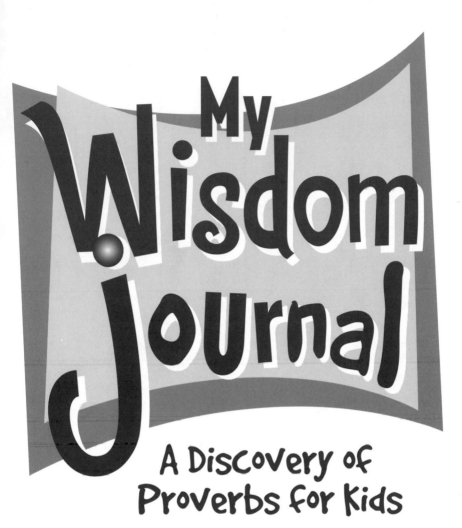

My Wisdom Journal

A Discovery of Proverbs for Kids

Mary J. Davis

D0012584

To all the students at Keokuk Christian Academy:
Keep striving to learn God's wisdom.

Also, to my family.

MY WISDOM JOURNAL
©2000 by Legacy Press, second printing
ISBN 1-885358-73-3

Legacy reorder #LP46941

Illustrator: Barbara Rodgers
Editor: Christy Allen

Legacy Press
P.O. Box 261129
San Diego, CA 91296

Printed in the United States of America

Table of Contents

Introduction

Have you ever wondered if you were doing wrong by fighting with a friend? Did you ever feel bad after gossiping about someone? What does God's Word have to say about your tongue or your heart?

The Bible's book of Proverbs answers many of the questions you might have about how God wants you to live. Wisdom ("understanding what is true, right or lasting") and encouragement for right-living are the main messages of Proverbs.

You will read lots of tasty tidbits in Proverbs. That is why you will find that the headings in each lesson offer you a morsel. By the time you finish *My Wisdom Journal*, you will be full of Proverbs' morsels.

To make the best use of this journal, follow these steps:

Morsel to Remember

These are good verses to memorize. Keep these positive Scriptures in your heart and mind.

Morsels of Wisdom

Read these verses before going on.

Morsels of Reflection

Here you will find explanations of the verses you just read, and questions that will help you think more about each verse.

Morsels of Prayer

These are suggested prayers, but you can make up your own prayers, too. You may pray before, during or after your journaling.

Feast on the Word

This section lists half of a Proverbs chapter to read. If you read the assigned half-chapter each time you use this journal, you will complete the entire book of Proverbs. Use the lines underneath the Scripture reference to jot down a favorite verse and what you learned in your reading.

Wisdom

Purpose Of This Book

Morsel to Remember

8/17

Listen, my son, to your father's instruction and do not forsake your mother's teaching. They will be a garland to grace your head and a chain to adorn your neck.

Proverbs 1:8-9

Morsels Of Wisdom

Proverbs 1:1-6 — (1) The proverbs of Solomon son of David, king of Israel: (2) for attaining wisdom and discipline; for understanding words of insight; (3) for acquiring a disciplined and prudent life, doing what is right and just and fair; (4) for giving prudence to the simple, knowledge and discretion to the young — (5) let the wise listen and add to their learning, and let the discerning get guidance — (6) for understanding proverbs and parables, the sayings and riddles of the wise.

Proverbs 2:6 — For the Lord gives wisdom, and from his mouth come knowledge and understanding.

Proverbs 24:3-5 — (3) By wisdom a house is built, and through understanding it is established; (4) through knowledge its rooms are filled with rare and beautiful treasures. (5) A wise man has great power, and a man of knowledge increases strength.

Morsels Of Reflection

Read the definition of wisdom in the introduction on page 5. **Read 1:1-6 again.** Write out **1:2.**

(1.) The proverbs of Solomon son of David king of Israel (2) for attaining wisdom and discipline; for understanding words of insight

In verse 3, we are told the book will teach us to do what is ___right___ , ___just___ and ___fair___ .

Read 2:6 again. Where does wisdom come from?
___The Lord gives wisdom.___

What other two things come from this source? ___knowledge___
and ___understanding___

Look at the verses at the left again. Underline these words:
wisdom, wise, understanding, knowledge, discipline.

How can you use the wisdom you from Proverbs in your life?
___You can use it by a house that is built___
___through understanding, and established___
_____

Morsels of Prayer

God, I love to read Your Word. It is so exciting to read things
that I know I can use in my own life today. Thank You for Your
Word. Amen.

Feast on the Word

Read **Proverbs 1:1-19.**

What I learned: ___Knowledge begins with___
___respect for the Lord. Do not follow___
___the sinners and do not do what they do.___

My favorite verse: ___Knowledge begins with___
___respect for the Lord.___

Benefits of Wisdom

Morsel to Remember

But whoever listens to me will live in safety and be at ease, without fear of harm.

Proverbs 1:33

Morsels of Wisdom

Proverbs 2:1-5 — My son, if you accept my words and store up my commands within you, turning your ear to wisdom and applying your heart to understanding, and if you call out for insight and cry aloud for understanding, and if you look for it as for silver and search for it as for hidden treasure, then you will understand the fear of the Lord.

Proverbs 2:12 — Wisdom will save you from the ways of wicked men, from men whose words are perverse.

Proverbs 28:26 — He who trusts in himself is a fool, but he who walks in wisdom is kept safe.

Morsels of Reflection

Although the book of Proverbs uses the term "my son" a lot, read at it as "my child." God wants all of His children to have wisdom. He is not talking just to boys or men, but to girls and women, too!

Look at **2:1-5** above. Write two or three words that complete each phrase:

Accept _____

Store _____

Turning _____

Applying _____

Call _____

Cry _____

Look _____

Understand _____

In **2:12**, what does wisdom save you from? _The ways_
of a wicked men.

Write about a time when knowing God's Word kept you from
doing something wrong. _When a boy got teased by_
other people I said "This boy should
be treated better, he should not be teased.
What do you think "perverse words" means?
Wicked words

_____

Read 28:26 again. Why do you think God wants you to read this
verse?
God doesn't want me to walk in sight, but
walk in faith and wisdom.
How can someone who trusts in herself be foolish?
She is foolish because she walking
in sight.

Morsels of Prayer

Father, I know that learning wisdom and understanding how
to follow Your ways will keep me out of trouble. Thank You for
giving me the desire to gain Your wisdom. Amen.

Feast on the Word

Read **Proverbs 1:20-33.**

What I learned: _Wisdom is like a good women_
who shout in the streets. She rasies her
vocie in the city square. Those who listen
to me will be safe, without fear of being hurt.
My favorite verse:
Proverbs 1: 33 Those who listen to Me will live in
safety. They will be safe, without
fear of being hurt

Gain Wisdom

Morsel to Remember

For the Lord gives wisdom, and from his mouth come knowledge and understanding.

Proverbs 2:6

Morsels of Wisdom

Proverbs 1:8 — Listen, my son, to your father's instruction and do not forsake your mother's teaching.

Proverbs 3:13 — Blessed is the man who finds wisdom, the man who gains understanding.

Proverbs 4:1 — Pay attention and gain understanding.

Proverbs 7:1 — Store up my commands within you.

Proverbs 7:2 — Keep my commands and you will live.

Morsels of Reflection

Read all of the verses above. List at least three ways to gain wisdom.

pay attention to the Lord, keep his commands, listen to my father's instruction

What important truth has your father or mother taught you that you will never forget?

Telling the turth

How has this helped you be a better Christian?

It told me that being thurful will make me a good Chirstian.

How would you explain wisdom to a friend?

Wisdom is a gift that you deserve.

If your friend asked you how to gain wisdom, how would you answer that question?

Obey our parents, remember their
teaching

Write the first two words of **3:13** on each of the lines below.

Blessed

_is_

Then write some words from each of the other verses to tell how to be blessed by God.

Listen, obey, remember, store, keep

Morsels of Prayer

God, I promise to work hard at listening, paying attention, gaining wisdom and storing up Your commands to live a better life for You. Amen.

Feast on the Word

Read **Proverbs 2:1-11.**

What I learned: _how God protects me,_
know him better, and to what
is good, bad

My favorite verse: _Good sense will protect_
me. Understanding will guard me.

Rejecting Wisdom

Morsel to Remember

The fear of the Lord is the beginning of knowledge.

Proverbs 1:7

Morsels of Wisdom

Proverbs 1:28-29 — Then they will call to me but I will not answer; they will look for me but will not find me. Since they hated knowledge and did not choose to fear the Lord.

Proverbs 5:21 — A man's ways are in full view of the Lord, and he examines all his paths.

Proverbs 12:1 — Whoever loves discipline loves knowledge [wisdom], but he who hates correction is stupid.

Proverbs 15:10 — Stern discipline awaits him who leaves the path.

Morsels of Reflection

Read 1:28 again. Who do you think will call to God and He will not answer? What do you think it would be like to look for God or call for God and not be able to find Him?

People do not listen to him, If I lookin for God and did not find Him, I would keepn look for it.

Read 5:21 again. Do you have a place you can go to be completely alone?

I don't have a place to be alone.

Are there times you do, see, say or think things that you know God would not approve of?

Yes, like sometimes I ask him to forgive me I don't feel it or when I ask to heal my face it does not get better.

Can you hide these things from God, even in your own private place at home?

I can not hide anything from God

Read 12:1 again. Think of a time when you have done something that you know is wrong. How did you feel when your parents found out and you were punished? What did you learn from it?

I felt sacred and painful. I learned to never do it again.

Read 15:10 again. Sometimes you might do something wrong but nobody ever finds out. Does God know?

God know everything what I have done.

What do you think this verse means?

Disapline wait for us when we leave the path.

Morsels of Prayer

Lord, I don't want to reject Your wisdom, knowledge or correction. I want to do my best for You all my life. You see everything I do, know everything I think and hear everything I say. I know that someone around me might see me do wrong and think it is okay to do wrong. Help me to be a good Christian and a good witness to those around me. Amen.

Feast on the Word

Read **Proverbs 2:12-22.**

What I learned: *God knows everything and keep my promise to God,*

My favorite verse: *wisdom will help me be a good person. It will help me do what is right.*

Fools and Their Folly

Morsel to Remember

Trust in the Lord with all your heart and lean not on your own understanding.

Proverbs 3:5

Morsels of Wisdom

Proverbs 10:23 — A fool finds pleasure in evil conduct, but a man of understanding delights in wisdom.

Proverbs 12:15 — The way of a fool seems right to him, but a wise man listens to advice.

Proverbs 14:24 — The wealth of the wise is their crown, but the folly of fools yields folly.

Proverbs 15:2 — The tongue of the wise commends knowledge, but the mouth of the fool gushes folly.

Morsels of Reflection

Did you ever try to convince a friend to not do something she knows is wrong?

_____

_____

Did someone ever try to give you advice but you just went right ahead and sinned?

_____

_____

Read verse 12:15, then 10:23. Write about a time when you made yourself believe that doing something wrong really wasn't wrong at all. What happened?

_____

_____

Read 14:24 and 15:2 again. On a separate sheet of paper, draw a picture of someone who is foolish. Then write verse **14:24** on the paper. Put your picture where you can see if often.

Morsels of Prayer

Lord, I don't want to be a foolish person. I know sometimes I do things that don't make sense. But, after I do these things, it is too late to go back and undo them. Help me to stop and think before I do things that would not be approved by You.

Feast in the Word

Read **Proverbs 3:1-16.**

What I learned: _____

_____

_____

My favorite verse: _____

The Righteous

The Righteous

Morsel to Remember

By wisdom the Lord laid the earth's foundations, by understanding he set the heavens in place; by his knowledge the deeps were divided, and the clouds let drop the dew.

Proverbs 3:19-20

Morsels of Wisdom

Proverbs 8:20 — I walk in the way of righteousness, along the paths of justice.

Proverbs 13:5 — The righteous hate what is false.

Proverbs 29:7 — The righteous care about justice for the poor.

Proverbs 29:27 — The righteous detest the dishonest.

Morsels of Reflection

An easy way to remember what righteousness means is to shorten the word to "rightness." Of course, the righteous do not do wrong things. They follow God's Word and do what pleases God.

Read all of the verses to see some of the things the righteous do, then list two or more things you can work on in your life to be more righteous.

_____

_____

On a separate piece of paper, draw two simple maps: one of your home and the other of your school. Along the pathways of the map, write ways to be more righteous. Example: Respect my teacher.

Morsels of Prayer

God, I want to be more righteous. I know that the way to be better at anything is to practice. Help me to practice righteousness (rightness) in all I do. Amen.

Feast on the Word

Read **Proverbs 3:17-35.**

What I learned: _____

_____

_____

My favorite verse: _____

Rewards and Blessings of the Righteous

Morsel to Remember

Hold on to instruction, do not let it go; guard it well, for it is your life.

Proverbs 4:13

Morsels of Wisdom

Proverbs 3:33 — The Lord's curse is on the house of the wicked, but he blesses the home of the righteous.

Proverbs 10:6 — Blessings crown the head of the righteous, but violence overwhelms the mouth of the wicked.

Proverbs 11:19 — The truly righteous man attains life, but he who pursues evil goes to his death.

Proverbs 13:9 — The light of the righteous shines brightly, but the lamp of the wicked is snuffed out.

Proverbs 28:20 — A faithful man will be richly blessed.

Morsels of Reflection

Read all of the verses above. Write some of the good things that are rewards for the righteous.

_____

_____

List some blessings that you have. Example: A good home.

_____

_____

Now, write how you would feel if those things were taken away from you.

_____

_____

Write out verse **28:20.**

_____

_____

Morsels of Prayer

God, I thank You for all of the blessings in my life. I am truly blessed and rich in wonderful things. Help me to be a righteous person and to always be thankful for my blessings. Amen.

Feast on the Word

Read **Proverbs 4:1-14.**

What I learned: _____

_____

_____

My favorite verse: _____

Faithfulness

The Faithful

Morsel to Remember

Make level paths for your feet and take only ways that are firm. Do not swerve to the right or the left; keep your foot from evil.

Proverbs 4:26-27

Morsels of Wisdom

Proverbs 2:8 — For he guards the course of the just and protects the way of his faithful ones.

Proverbs 28:20 — A faithful man will be richly blessed.

Proverbs 31:26 — She speaks with wisdom, and faithful instruction is on her tongue.

Morsels of Reflection

Faithful means someone who has faith. It also means someone who is worthy of trust. Both of these meanings are important when you think of your relationship with God. You have faith in God, and know that He will take care of you. On the other hand, you have to be worthy of God's and people's trust in you. You cannot be dishonest, hurtful, hateful and unreliable.

Write out **31:26.**

_____

_____

_____

Write a few sentences about someone you know who is like that verse. How can you become more like that person?

_____

_____

_____

Morsels of Prayer

Father, I want to be the type of person that others will want to be like. I want it to be said of me that I speak with wisdom and faithful instruction, rather than bad things. Help me to be worthy of Your trust in me. Amen.

Feast on the Word

Read **Proverbs 4:15-27.**

What I learned: _____

_____

_____

My favorite verse: _____

Faithfulness

Morsel to Remember

Let love and faithfulness never leave you; bind them around your neck, write them on the tablet of your heart.

Proverbs 3:3

Pay attention to my wisdom, listen well to my words of insight.

Proverbs 5:1

Morsels of Wisdom

Proverbs 3:3 — Let love and faithfulness never leave you; bind them around your neck, write them on the tablet of your heart.

Proverbs 14:22 — Do not those who plot evil go astray? But those who plan what is good find love and faithfulness.

Proverbs 16:6 — Through love and faithfulness sin is atoned for.

Proverbs 20:28 — Love and faithfulness keep a king safe; through love his throne is made secure.

Morsels of Reflection

These verses speak of faithfulness with love. God wants you to know that love and faithfulness go hand in hand. If you love God, you will be faithful.

Read 3:3 again. Cut out a paper heart. Write the verse on the heart, and place it where you can see it often.

Read 14:22 again. Write a story about someone who plans something bad, such as stealing something, then does it more and more. Write the verse, 14:22, at the end of the story.

_____

_____

_____

Read 16:6 and 20:28 again. How can each of these verses help you stay faithful in the Lord?

_____

_____

Morsel of Prayer

Dear God, I want to remember to keep love and faithfulness in my heart and mind. Then my actions will show love and faithfulness in all that I do. Amen.

Feast on the Word

Read **Proverbs 5:1-12.**

What I learned: _____

_____

_____

My favorite verse: _____

The Unfaithful

Morsel to Remember

For a man's ways are in full view of the Lord, and he examines all his paths.

Proverbs 5:21

Morsels of Wisdom

Proverbs 11:3 — The integrity of the upright guides them, but the unfaithful are destroyed by their duplicity. [Integrity means being morally upright or honest. Duplicity means being deceptive or dishonest.]

Proverbs 11:6 — The righteousness of the upright delivers them, but the unfaithful are trapped by evil desires.

Proverbs 13:15 — Good understanding wins favor, but the way of the unfaithful is hard.

Proverbs 22:12 — The eyes of the Lord keep watch over knowledge, but he frustrates the words of the unfaithful.

Morsels of Reflection

Is there someone you know, whom you do not fully trust? Have your parents warned you against hanging around a certain person at school? You can usually tell whether to trust people by the way they act. You can tell that people are morally upright by the way they talk, treat other people and act like godly people.

Write what each verse says about the unfaithful.

_____

_____

_____

_____

Doesn't this seem like a lonely and hard way to go through life? Especially when all you have to do is become a child of God and follow His ways!

Write a prayer to ask God to help you be an upright and faithful person.

_____

_____

_____

_____

Morsels of Prayer

Father, I love You, and I love Your ways. Help me to be faithful to You all my life. Amen.

Feast on the Word

Read **Proverbs 5:13-23.**

What I learned: _____

_____

_____

My favorite verse: _____

Trust

Morsel to Remember

Whoever gives heed to instruction prospers, and blessed is he who trusts in the Lord.

Proverbs 16:20

Morsels of Wisdom

Proverbs 3:5 — Trust in the Lord with all your heart and lean not on your own understanding.

Proverbs 16:20 — Blessed is he who trusts in the Lord.

Proverbs 24:10 — If you falter in times of trouble, how small is your strength!

Morsels of Reflection

Write about a time when you were really afraid. How did God carry you through that time?

_____

_____

Read verses 3:5 and 16:20 again.

Read verse 24:10 again. Write a pretend letter to tell a friend how to trust in God and not falter. (Verses 3:5 and 16:20 contain some good words to use.)

_____

_____

_____

_____

_____

_____

Morsels of Prayer

Dear Lord, I am sometimes afraid or worried. Help me to lean on You and trust You with all my heart. I love You, Lord. Amen.

Feast on the Word

Read **Proverbs 16:1-19.**

What I learned: _____

_____

_____

My favorite verse: _____

Fear of God

Morsel to Remember

My son, keep your father's commands and do not forsake your mother's teaching. Bind them upon your heart forever; fasten them around your neck. When you walk, they will guide you; when you sleep, they will watch over you; when you awake, they will speak to you. For these commands are a lamp, this teaching is a light.

Proverbs 6:20-23

Morsels of Wisdom

Proverbs 1:7 — The fear of the Lord is the beginning of knowledge.

Proverbs 3:7 — Do not be wise in your own eyes; fear the Lord and shun evil.

Proverbs 9:10 — The fear of the Lord is the beginning of wisdom, and knowledge of the Holy One is understanding.

Proverbs 10:27 — The fear of the Lord adds length to life.

Proverbs 14:27 — The fear of the Lord is a fountain of life.

Proverbs 15:33 — The fear of the Lord teaches a man wisdom, and humility comes before honor.

Proverbs 16:6 — Through love and faithfulness sin is atoned for; through the fear of the Lord a man avoids evil.

Morsels of Reflection

Read all the verses above. Write at least three good things that fear of the Lord will bring to you.

_____

_____

Why do you think that fearing God is a good thing?

_____

_____

Read again and write out Proverbs 16:6. Do you think that God wants you to be afraid of Him, or to fear His punishment if you do not obey His commands?

_____

_____

List some things that you are afraid of.

_____

_____

_____

Read the verses at left. Why is the fear of God different than the things you listed?

_____

_____

Morsels of Prayer

God, I love You, and I know You love me. I know that fearing You is not the same as being afraid of something harmful. You want me to be afraid of disappointing You, so that I can live a godly life. Amen.

Feast on the Word

Read **Proverbs 6:20-35.**

What I learned: _____

_____

_____

My favorite verse: _____

Hope

Hope

Morsel to Remember

Guard my teachings as the apple of your eye.

Proverbs 7:2

Morsels of Wisdom

Proverbs 19:18 — Discipline your son, for in that there is hope; do not be a willing party to his death.

Proverbs 23:18 — There is surely a future hope for you, and your hope will not be cut off.

Proverbs 24:14 — Know also that wisdom is sweet to your soul; if you find it, there is a future hope for you, and your hope will not be cut off.

Morsels of Reflection

Read 19:18 again. Why do you think death is mentioned in this verse?

_____

_____

What do you think would happen if parents did not discipline their children?

_____

_____

What do you think the world would be like if God did not discipline His people?

_____

_____

Read 23:18 and 24:14 again. List at least three things you hope for in your future.

_____

If you have wisdom and follow God's ways, you have the hope of spending eternity in heaven with God. Write an advertisement to convince people to gain wisdom and have the hope of heaven.

_____

_____

Morsels of Prayer

God, You give me a hope that nobody else could ever give me. I know that I will spend my eternity in heaven with You. Thank You for that hope. It makes even my darkest days look bright. I love You, God! Amen.

Feast on the Word

Read **Proverbs 7:1-13.**

What I learned: _____

_____

_____

My favorite verse: _____

No Hope for the Wicked

Morsel to Remember

Say to wisdom, "You are my sister."

Proverbs 7:4

Morsels of Wisdom

Proverbs 11:7 — When a wicked man dies, his hope perishes; all he expected from his power comes to nothing.

Proverbs 11:23 — The desire of the righteous ends only in good, but the hope of the wicked only in wrath.

Proverbs 24:20 — For the evil man has no future hope, and the lamp of the wicked will be snuffed out.

Morsels of Reflection

Have you ever heard this expression: "You can't take your money with you when you die"?

Read verse 11:7 again. Write out what you think that means.

_____

_____

Read 11:23 again. The first part of the verse is a happy thought, while the second part is quite different. How does this verse make you want to live your life?

_____

_____

Read 24:20 again. Does the evil man have any future hope? What will happen to the lamp (hope) of the wicked?

_____

_____

Write this phrase on at least three pieces of paper: I have hope. Put the papers in places where you can see them many times each day.

Pray for someone who needs to know God.

Morsels of Prayer

Dear God, I am glad I'm not one who has no hope. I am thankful to be Your child. Help me to introduce someone to You, so that he or she will also have hope. Amen.

Feast on the Word

Read **Proverbs 7:14-27.**

What I learned: _____

_____

_____

My favorite verse: _____

Love

God Loves Me

Morsel to Remember

Choose my instruction instead of silver, knowledge rather than choice gold, for wisdom is more precious than rubies, and nothing you desire can compare with her.

Proverbs 8:10-11

Morsels of Wisdom

Proverbs 3:12 — The Lord disciplines those he loves.

Proverbs 8:17 — I love those who love me, and those who seek me find me.

Proverbs 8:20-21 — I walk in the way of righteousness, along the paths of justice, bestowing wealth on those who love me and making their treasuries full.

Morsels of Reflection

Read 3:12 again. When has God disciplined you or made you feel guilty for some wrong you have done?

_____

_____

Do you think God would have done this if He didn't care about you?

_____

_____

Read 8:17 again. In what ways can we seek God?

_____

_____

Read 8:21 again. Do you think this means God will make you rich if you believe in Him?

_____

_____

What do you think it means?

_____

_____

List at least five blessings God has given you. Why do you think God has blessed you with these things?

_____

_____

Write a poem to tell God you love Him.

_____

_____

Morsels of Prayer

God, I love You, not only because You loved me first. You are awesome! You mean everything to me. Amen.

Feast on the Word

Read **Proverbs 8:1-18**.

What I learned: _____

_____

_____

My favorite verse: _____

Love Others

Morsel to Remember

A friend loves at all times.

Proverbs 17:17

Morsels of Wisdom

Proverbs 3:3 — Let love and faithfulness never leave you; bind them around your neck, write them on the tablet of your heart.

Proverbs 10:12 — Hatred stirs up dissension, but love covers over all wrongs.

Proverbs 17:9 — He who covers over an offense promotes love, but whoever repeats the matter separates close friends.

Proverbs 17:17 — A friend loves at all times.

Proverbs 21:21 — He who pursues righteousness and love finds life, prosperity and honor.

Morsels of Reflection

Read all of the verses again. When should a friend love?

_____

_____

Should you ever NOT have love?

_____

_____

What does love cover?

_____

_____

What can separate close friends?

_____

Write out verse 21:21.

_____

_____

Write about a time when you and a friend were not speaking to each other. How could you have made the situation better?

_____

_____

Morsels of Prayer

Lord, I know You want me to love everyone. I know I sometimes am not very good at that. Help me to show love even to those who do things to upset me. Amen.

Feast on the Word

Read **Proverbs 8:19-36.**

What I learned: _____

_____

_____

My favorite verse: _____

Honesty

Honesty vs. Dishonesty

Morsel to Remember

An honest answer is like a kiss on the lips.

Proverbs 24:26

Morsels of Wisdom

Proverbs 11:1 — The Lord abhors dishonest scales, but accurate weights are his delight.

Proverbs 13:11 — Dishonest money dwindles away, but he who gathers money little by little makes it grow.

Proverbs 16:11 — Honest scales and balances are from the Lord.

Proverbs 20:23 — The Lord detests differing weights, and dishonest scales do not please him.

Proverbs 29:27 — The righteous detest the dishonest.

Morsels of Reflection

Read 16:11, 11:1 and 20:23 again. These verses tell how to deal with people around you. If you cheat people, you are dishonest. Write one instance where you might be tempted to cheat someone. Example: A grocery store clerk accidentally gives you back $5 too much.

_____

_____

Read verse 13:11 again. If you gained money dishonestly, how would it make you feel to be reminded of your dishonesty every time you spent some of the money?

_____

_____

Read 29:27 again. This doesn't mean you should hate anyone. What do you think it does mean?

_____

_____

Write out the memory verse, **Proverbs 24:26**.

_____

_____

Write another sentence to describe what honesty is like.

_____

_____

Morsels of Prayer

Father, I understand how important it is to be honest. I don't want to cheat anyone. I don't want to do anything to make others think I am not a child of God. Help me to deal honestly with all those around me. Amen.

Feast on the Word

Read **Proverbs 9:1-18.**

What I learned: _____

_____

_____

My favorite verse: _____

Truth vs. Lies

Morsel to Remember

The Lord detests lying lips, but he delights in men who are truthful.

Proverbs 12:22

Morsels of Wisdom

Proverbs 12:17 — A truthful witness gives honest testimony, but a false witness tells lies.

Proverbs 12:19 — Truthful lips endure forever, but a lying tongue lasts only a moment.

Proverbs 12:22 — The Lord detests lying lips, but he delights in men who are truthful.

Proverbs 14:5 — A truthful witness does not deceive, but a false witness pours out lies.

Proverbs 19:5 — A false witness will not go unpunished, and he who pours out lies will not go free.

Proverbs 19:9 — A false witness will not go unpunished, and he who pours out lies will perish.

Morsels of Reflection

What does a false witness do?

_____

_____

What only lasts a moment?

_____

_____

What endures forever?

_____

_____

How does God feel about lying lips?

_____

_____

Finish this sentence: He who pours out lies will not go
_____and will_____.

Do you know someone who does not tell the truth? As a child
of God, you do not want to get that kind of reputation. You
want to be known as someone who always is truthful and
trustworthy.

Morsels of Prayer

God, it is so easy sometimes to tell a little lie. It is sometimes
embarrassing to tell the entire truth. Help me to realize that it is
much more important to tell the truth than to save myself a
little embarrassment. Amen.

Feast on the Word

Read **Proverbs 10:1-16**.

What I learned: _____

_____

_____

My favorite verse: _____

What God Hates

Morsel to Remember

The tongue of the righteous is choice silver, but the heart of the wicked is of little value. The lips of the righteous nourish many, but fools die for lack of judgment.

Proverbs 10:20-21

Morsels of Wisdom

Proverbs 6:16-19 — (16) There are six things the Lord hates, seven that are detestable to him: (17) haughty eyes, a lying tongue, hands that shed innocent blood, (18) a heart that devises wicked schemes, feet that are quick to rush into evil, (19) a false witness who pours out lies and a man who stirs up dissension among brothers.

Morsels of Reflection

The verses above do not paint a very pretty picture, do they?

Write the seven things that God detests:

1. _____

2. _____

3. _____

4. _____

5. _____

6. _____

7. _____

Write how you can make sure you aren't doing these things.

_____

_____

Do you know someone who is like the person in the last half of verse 19? This person is always stirring up trouble between people. What could you say to this person to help her understand the problems and trouble she causes?

_____

_____

Morsels of Prayer

I don't want to be any of these things, Lord. Help me to put only good things into my walk with You. Help me to be a positive person and a good friend to others. Amen.

Feast on the Word

Read **Proverbs 10:17-32**.

What I learned: _____

_____

_____

My favorite verse: _____

Teachings

Parent Teachings

Morsel to Remember

Through the blessing of the upright a city is exalted, but by the mouth of the wicked it is destroyed.

Proverbs 11:11

Morsels of Wisdom

Proverbs 1:8-9 — Listen, my son [child], to your father's instruction and do not forsake your mother's teaching. They will be a garland to grace your head and a chain to adorn your neck.

Proverbs 3:1-2 — My son [child], do not forget my teaching, but keep my commands in your heart, for they will prolong your life many years and bring you prosperity.

Proverbs 4:1 — Listen, my sons [children], to a father's instruction; pay attention and gain understanding.

Proverbs 4:2 — I give you sound learning, so do not forsake my teaching.

Proverbs 6:20-21 — My son [child], keep your father's commands and do not forsake your mother's teaching. Bind them upon your heart forever; fasten them around your neck.

Morsels of Reflection

Whom do you think God has given you to teach you His ways?

_____

_____

What are some of the benefits of listening to your parents' teachings?

_____

_____

Read 3:1 and 6:21 again. Where should you keep God's commands?

_____

Write a letter to your parents and thank them for teaching you to be the best you can be for God.

_____

_____

Write a letter to a favorite Sunday school teacher or pastor and thank this person for all he or she has taught you.

_____

_____

Morsels of Prayer

God, you set up a wonderful system. Our parents learned from their parents and they learned from their parents, just as I will learn from my parents and in turn teach my children. Thank You for giving me someone to teach me how to be the best I can be for You. Amen.

Feast on the Word

Read **Proverbs 11:1-15.**

What I learned: _____

_____

_____

My favorite verse: _____

God's Teachings

Morsel to Remember

The teaching of the wise is a fountain of life, turning a man from the snares of death.

Proverbs 13:14

Morsels of Wisdom

Proverbs 2:6 — For the Lord gives wisdom.

Proverbs 7:2 — Keep my commands and you will live; guard my teachings as the apple of your eye.

Proverbs 13:14 — The teaching of the wise is a fountain of life, turning a man from the snares of death.

Proverbs 22:20-21 — Have I not written thirty sayings for you, sayings of counsel and knowledge, teaching you true and reliable words, so that you can give sound answers to him who sent you?

Morsels of Reflection

Who gives wisdom?

_____

_____

What is the fountain of life?

_____

_____

Write what you think wisdom does to help you live for God.

_____

_____

Write a paragraph to a younger person to encourage him or her to keep God's commands and learn to walk in God's ways.

_____

_____

Morsels of Prayer

God, I am so glad that Your book is filled with wonderful advice on how to be a godly person. I want to be the best I can be for You. I love You. Amen.

Feast on the Word

Read **Proverbs 11:16-31.**

What I learned: _____

_____

_____

My favorite verse: _____

Instruction

Morsel to Remember

Whoever gives heed to instruction prospers, and blessed is he who trusts in the Lord. The wise in heart are called discerning, and pleasant words promote instruction. Understanding is a fountain of life to those who have it, but folly brings punishment to fools. A wise man's heart guides his mouth, and his lips promote instruction.

Proverbs 16:20-23

Morsels of Wisdom

Proverbs 4:13 — Hold on to instruction, do not let it go; guard it well, for it is your life.

Proverbs 8:10 — Choose my instruction instead of silver, knowledge rather than choice gold.

Proverbs 8:33 — Listen to my instruction and be wise; do not ignore it.

Proverbs 13:13 — He who scorns instruction will pay for it, but he who respects a command is rewarded.

Proverbs 19:20 — Listen to advice and accept instruction, and in the end you will be wise.

Morsels of Reflection

What do you think instruction means?

_____

_____

What is it that you need to learn about?

_____

_____

Write out **19:20.**

_____

_____

Write about a time when you should have listened to God's Word and done something differently.

_____

_____

How will you do differently next time the same situation comes up?

_____

_____

Morsels of Prayer

Lord, I want to hold on to all Your instruction. I know it is very important for me to follow Your commands. Please forgive me for the things I've done wrong and the bad choices I have made. Help me to do better. Amen.

Feast on the Word

Read **Proverbs 12:1-14.**

What I learned: _____

_____

_____

My favorite verse: _____

correction

Morsel to Remember

Train a child in the way he should go, and when he is old he will not turn from it.

Proverbs 22:6

Morsels of Wisdom

Proverbs 6:23 — The corrections of discipline are the way to life.

Proverbs 13:18 — He who ignores discipline comes to poverty and shame, but whoever heeds correction is honored.

Proverbs 13:24 — He who spares the rod hates his son, but he who loves him is careful to discipline him.

Proverbs 19:18 — Discipline your son, for in that there is hope.

Morsels of Reflection

How do your parents discipline you?

_____

_____

How do you think God disciplines you?

_____

_____

You can take comfort in the thought that even adults are disciplined by God.

Read 6:23 and 13:18 again. Why do you think God wants parents to discipline their children?

_____

_____

Write out 19:18 and 22:6.

_____

_____

Morsels of Prayer

God I know You want me to obey Your commands and live in the ways You tell us in the Bible. I like the verse that says "train up a child in the way he should go." Even if no one in my family is a Christian, I can still learn Your ways by reading the Bible and going to church or Sunday school. Help me to be all I can for You, God. Amen.

Feast on the Word

Read **Proverbs 12:15-28.**

What I learned: _____

_____

_____

My favorite verse: _____

sin

Temptation

Morsel to Remember

A righteous man is cautious in friendship.

Proverbs 12:26

Morsels of Wisdom

Proverbs 1:10-16 — My son [child], if sinners entice you, do not give in to them. If they say, "Come along with us; let's lie in wait for someone's blood, let's waylay some harmless soul; let's swallow them alive, like the grave, and whole, like those who go down to the pit; we will get all sorts of valuable things and fill our houses with plunder; throw in your lot with us, and we will share a common purse" — my son [child], do not go along with them, do not set foot on their paths; for their feet rush into sin.

Morsels of Reflection

Following the crowd is usually not the right thing to do. However, you might be afraid to stand up to someone who is leading you down the wrong path. How does God feel about His children following along with wrongdoers?

_____

_____

What do you suppose God wants you to do when someone tries to get you to follow along?

_____

_____

Write out the memory verse.

_____

_____

What do you think it means?

_____

_____

Morsels of Prayer

God, I sometimes let my friends make decisions for me. Those decisions are not always the right choices. Please help me to stand up for what is right! Amen.

Feast on the Word

Read **Proverbs 13:1-12.**

What I learned: _____

_____

_____

My favorite verse: _____

Evil

Morsel to Remember

If a man pays back evil for good, evil will never leave his house.

Proverbs 17:13

Morsels of Wisdom

Proverbs 3:33 — The Lord's curse is on the house of the wicked, but he blesses the home of the righteous.

Proverbs 11:7-8 — When a wicked man dies, his hope perishes; all he expected from his power comes to nothing. The righteous man is rescued from trouble, and it comes on the wicked instead.

Proverbs 12:20 — There is deceit in the hearts of those who plot evil, but joy for those who promote peace.

Proverbs 14:19 — Evil men will bow down in the presence of the good, and the wicked at the gates of the righteous.

Proverbs 21:10 — The wicked man craves evil; his neighbor gets no mercy from him.

Morsels of Reflection

Read 3:33 again. Would you want to live without God's blessings?

_____

_____

How can you have God's blessings?

_____

_____

Read 11:7-8. again What happens to the wicked?

_____

_____

Read the remaining verses again. Write one thing you learned in the verses.

_____

_____

Write what you think an evil or wicked person is, what this kind of person does and how God feels about the wicked person.

_____

_____

Morsels of Prayer

God, I don't want to be an evil person. I love You, and I love Your ways. Help me to follow You all my life. Amen.

Feast on the Word

Read **Proverbs 13:13-25.**

What I learned: _____

_____

_____

My favorite verse: _____

Hate Evil

Morsel to Remember

A wise man fears the Lord and shuns evil.

Proverbs 14:16

Morsels of Wisdom

Proverbs 8:13 — To fear the Lord is to hate evil; I hate pride and arrogance, evil behavior and perverse speech.

Proverbs 10:23 — A fool finds pleasure in evil conduct, but a man of understanding delights in wisdom.

Proverbs 10:29 — The way of the Lord is a refuge for the righteous, but it is the ruin of those who do evil.

Proverbs 21:27 — The sacrifice of the wicked is detestable — how much more so when brought with evil intent!

Morsels of Reflection

Read 8:13 again. What does God hate?

_____

_____

Read 10:23 again. A man of understanding loves wisdom. What does a fool love?

_____

_____

In **10:29,** what do you think refuge is?

_____

_____

Read 21:27 again. In the Old Testament, God commanded that the people bring sacrifices to atone for their sins. This verse says that God hates the sacrifices of evil people, even more so when they bring them to God without being sorry for their sins. How would you rewrite verse 21:27 for today? For example, you might write about going to church with an evil heart or hateful attitude.

_____

_____

Morsels of Prayer

Lord, I know You hate evil. I hate evil, too! Please help me to keep evil thoughts out of my mind and evil deeds out of my life. Amen.

Feast on the Word

Read **Proverbs 14:1-16.**

What I learned: _____

_____

_____

My favorite verse: _____

Avoid Evil

Morsel to Remember

Do not those who plot evil go astray? But those who plan what is good find love and faithfulness.

Proverbs 14:22

Morsels of Wisdom

Proverbs 2:12-16 — Wisdom will save you from the ways of wicked men, from men whose words are perverse, who leave the straight paths to walk in dark ways, who delight in doing wrong and rejoice in the perverseness of evil, whose paths are crooked and who are devious in their ways.

Proverbs 4:14 — Do not set foot on the path of the wicked or walk in the way of evil men.

Proverbs 4:27 — Do not swerve to the right or the left; keep your foot from evil.

Proverbs 16:17 — The highway of the upright avoids evil; he who guards his way guards his life.

Morsels of Reflection

Read 2:12-16 again. Write some things that the wicked do.

_____

_____

Trace your feet onto a piece of paper. Cut out both traced feet. Write verse **4:14** on one and verse **4:27** on the other. Place the feet where you can see the verses everyday. Remember to keep on God's path.

Read 16:17 again. Why do you think avoiding evil helps to guard your life?

_____

_____

Morsels of Prayer

Father, I will try very hard not to do any of those things that the wicked do. I want to follow You, not evil people. I want to follow Your straight path. Amen.

Feast on the Word

Read Proverbs 14:17-35.

What I learned: _____

_____

_____

My favorite verse: _____

Sinful Ways

Greed

Morsel to Remember

The eyes of the Lord are everywhere, keeping watch on the wicked and the good.

Proverbs 15:3

Morsels of Wisdom

Proverbs 15:27 — A greedy man brings trouble to his family, but he who hates bribes will live.

Proverbs 28:25 — A greedy man stirs up dissension, but he who trusts in the Lord will prosper.

Proverbs 29:4 — By justice a king gives a country stability, but one who is greedy for bribes tears it down.

Morsels of Reflection

What do you think greed is?

_____

_____

Greed can tear families apart. It can destroy friendships, businesses, governments and even churches. Greed drives people to dishonesty and to harm others just to gain more.

Read all of the verses above again. Who will prosper?

_____

_____

Make up a story about a mayor of a small town who was very greedy. What harm could come to the city in this situation?

_____

_____

_____

Morsels of Prayer

Lord, I don't think I am greedy. Help me not to envy what others have. Help me to remember that You provide everything that I need. Greed for money and possessions is not something a godly person should have. Amen.

Feast on the Word

Read **Proverbs 15:1-15.**

What I learned: _____

_____

_____

My favorite verse: _____

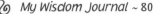

Anger

Morsel to Remember

A gentle answer turns away wrath, but a harsh word stirs up anger.

Proverbs 15:1

Morsels of Wisdom

Proverbs 29:8 — Mockers stir up a city, but wise men turn away anger.

Proverbs 29:11 — A fool gives full vent to his anger, but a wise man keeps himself under control.

Proverbs 30:33 — For as churning the milk produces butter, and as twisting the nose produces blood, so stirring up anger produces strife.

Morsels of Reflection

Read the memory verse. When have you used harsh words with someone? Write out a situation when you used words that you were sorry for later.

_____

_____

_____

_____

Read 29:8 again. Think about how the crowds turned against Jesus when only a few began to say bad things. What kind of situation could happen today, where a few people stirred up a whole crowd?

_____

_____

Read 30:33 again. It sounds like a riddle! Remember in Proverbs 1:6, where it says the Proverbs are the sayings and riddles of the wise? Write at least one riddle about what kind of trouble anger can cause.

_____

_____

Morsels of Prayer

Father, help me not to stir up anger. Help me to keep my hateful thoughts to myself and to not hurt the feelings of others. It is impossible to put words back into my mouth after I have said them. Help me not to let those words of anger slip out. Amen.

Feast on the Word

Read **Proverbs 15:16-33**.

What I learned: _____

_____

_____

My favorite verse: _____

My Temper

Morsel to Remember

Commit to the Lord whatever you do, and your plans will succeed.

Proverbs 16:3

Morsels of Wisdom

Proverbs 14:17 — A quick-tempered man does foolish things.

Proverbs 14:29 — A patient man has great understanding, but a quick-tempered man displays folly.

Proverbs 15:18 — A hot-tempered man stirs up dissension, but a patient man calms a quarrel.

Proverbs 16:32 — Better a patient man than a warrior, a man who controls his temper than one who takes a city.

Morsels of Reflection

God wants you to use patience in all situations. A person with a hot temper can quickly turn any situation into a bad one. **Read 14:17, 14:29 and 15:18. again** What kinds of things does a quick-tempered person do?

_____

_____

Read 16:32 again. A warrior is an honored person in Bible times. But this verse says that a person who can control his temper is even greater than a warrior.

Write about a time when you controlled your temper in a bad situation.

_____

_____

Write about a time when you did not control your temper.

_____

_____

Which way does God want you to be?

_____

_____

Morsels of Prayer

My temper sometimes gets in the way and gets me into trouble, God. Help me to control my temper. I want to be more like my Lord Jesus every day. Amen.

Feast on the Word

Read **Proverbs 16:1-16.**

What I learned: _____

_____

_____

My favorite verse: _____

Quarreling

Morsel to Remember

Pleasant words are a honeycomb, sweet to the soul and healing to the bones.

Proverbs 16:24

Morsels of Wisdom

Proverbs 13:10 — Pride only breeds quarrels.

Proverbs 15:18 — A patient man calms a quarrel.

Proverbs 17:14 — Starting a quarrel is like breaching a dam; so drop the matter before a dispute breaks out.

Proverbs 17:19 — He who loves a quarrel loves sin.

Proverbs 20:3 — It is to a man's honor to avoid strife, but every fool is quick to quarrel.

Morsels of Reflection

Do you find yourself quarreling with your brothers and sisters? Do you fight and argue with your best friend? Guess what? God wants you to stop quarreling! Verse 13:10 says that pride is often the cause of quarreling.

Read verse 15:18 again. How can you stop a quarrel?

_____

_____

Verse 17:14 tells another way to stop a quarrel. What is it?

_____

_____

If you love to quarrel, what do you love to do?

_____

_____

Read verse 20:3. It is an honorable thing in God's eyes to avoid strife and quarreling. Design a badge of honor below for someone who avoids quarreling.

Morsels of Prayer

Lord, I am guilty of quarreling. I fight with my brothers and sisters. I fight with my friends. I even fight with my parents. Help me to not be a quarreler. I know You don't like it, and it makes me upset after I've quarreled. I want to stop. Amen.

Feast on the Word

Read **Proverbs 16:17-33.**

What I learned: _____

_____

_____

My favorite verse.

_____

_____

Strife

Morsel to Remember

Better a dry crust with peace and quiet than a house full of feasting, with strife.

Proverbs 17:1

Morsels of Wisdom

Proverbs 10:12 — Hatred stirs up dissension, but love covers over all wrongs.

Proverbs 22:10 — Drive out the mocker, and out goes strife; quarrels and insults are ended.

Proverbs 26:21 — As charcoal to embers and as wood to fire, so is a quarrelsome man for kindling strife.

Morsels of Reflection

Strife and dissension mean disagreements, fighting and quarreling.

Read 10:12 again. What stirs up dissension?

_____

_____

What does love do?

_____

_____

Verse 22:10 says to get rid of the person who is stirring up trouble. This means not to hang around that kind of person. Do you have a friend who is always fighting with you or trying to get you to fight with others? God expects you to stay away from the situation. If you can't convince the friend to change her ways, then you should stay away from that person. Hanging around with the wrong people often gets us into situations that God doesn't approve of.

Read 26:21 again. How quickly wood is burned up in a fire! This verse says that a quarrelsome person can stir up trouble just as quickly.

Write a modern day proverb about strife and dissension. You may use the words quarreling, fighting, arguing or whatever words you want.

_____

_____

_____

Morsels of Prayer

God, I have a friend who always wants me to get in on fights and quarrels. I don't like it, but I am not sure how to get away from this friend. Would You help me to find some new friends? Amen.

Feast on the Word

Read **Proverbs 17:1-14.**

What I learned: _____

_____

_____

My favorite verse: _____

Jealousy

Morsel to Remember

A cheerful heart is good medicine, but a crushed spirit dries up the bones.

Proverbs 17:22

Morsels of Wisdom

Proverbs 3:31-32 — Do not envy a violent man or choose any of his ways.

Proverbs 23:17 — Do not let your heart envy sinners, but always be zealous for the fear of the Lord.

Proverbs 14:30 — A heart at peace gives life to the body, but envy rots the bones.

Proverbs 27:4 — Anger is cruel and fury overwhelming, but who can stand before jealousy?

Morsels of Reflection

Have your ever been jealous of someone? Do you get upset when someone at school seems to get all of the good stuff, and you don't? Does it make you angry when your best friend spends time with someone else?

Read 14:30 again. Think of how your heart feels when you are jealous of someone. Do you feel upset and almost sick? What does this verse say envy can do?

_____

_____

Read 3:31-32 and 23:17 again. Why do you suppose God doesn't want us to envy sinners?

_____

_____

How do you think sinners gain what they have?

_____

_____

Write out 27:4.

_____

_____

Anger and fury are really bad things, but God wants us to know that jealousy is even worse!

Write about someone you have been jealous of. What does he or she have that you want? Do you have something this person might be jealous of? Pray that God will help you not be jealous of anyone.

_____

_____

Morsels of Prayer

God, I sometimes envy what a friend has. But I realize I have much more than some people do. I am truly blessed. Please forgive me for the times when I forget how much You have done for me. Amen.

Feast on the Word

Read **Proverbs 17:15-28.**

What I learned: _____

_____

_____

My favorite verse: _____

Be careful

Pride vs. Humility

Morsel to Remember

The fear of the Lord teaches a man wisdom, and humility comes before honor.

Proverbs 15:33

Morsels of Wisdom

Proverbs 3:34 — He mocks proud mockers but gives grace to the humble.

Proverbs 11:2 — When pride comes, then comes disgrace, but with humility comes wisdom.

Proverbs 13:10 — Pride only breeds quarrels, but wisdom is found in those who take advice.

Proverbs 15:25 — The Lord tears down the proud man's house.

Proverbs 16:18-19 — Pride goes before destruction, a haughty spirit before a fall. Better to be lowly in spirit and among the oppressed than to share plunder with the proud.

Proverbs 18:12 — Before his downfall a man's heart is proud, but humility comes before honor.

Proverbs 22:4 — Humility and the fear of the Lord bring wealth and honor and life.

Morsels of Reflection

Someone who is humble, or has humility, is not prideful. List some of the bad things that can happen to those who are proud.

_____

_____

List the good things about having humility.

_____

_____

Write out verses 15:33 and 22:4 on a separate piece of paper. Put them where you can see them often. Memorize both verses.

Write about someone you have known who is very prideful. Pray for this person.

_____

_____

Morsels of Prayer

God, I hope I do not act proud and overconfident about everything. Please help me to be a humble person and to glorify You in all that I do. Amen.

Feast on the Word

Read **Proverbs 18:1-12.**

What I learned: _____

_____

_____

My favorite verse: _____

Riches

Morsel to Remember

Rich and poor have this in common: The Lord is the Maker of them all.
Proverbs 22:2

Morsels of Wisdom

Proverbs 11:28 — Whoever trusts in his riches will fall.

Proverbs 22:1 — A good name is more desirable than great riches; to be esteemed is better than silver or gold.

Proverbs 23:4-5 — Do not wear yourself out to get rich; have the wisdom to show restraint. Cast but a glance at riches, and they are gone, for they will surely sprout wings and fly off to the sky like an eagle.

Proverbs 27:24 — For riches do not endure forever, and a crown is not secure for all generations.

Proverbs 28:6 — Better a poor man whose walk is blameless than a rich man whose ways are perverse.

Proverbs 28:20 — A faithful man will be richly blessed, but one eager to get rich will not go unpunished.

Proverbs 28:22 — A stingy man is eager to get rich and is unaware that poverty awaits him.

Morsels of Reflection

How does God feel about rich people? It seems at first glance that He doesn't like them at all. However, read a little closer and you will find something else. What He is saying is that He doesn't want you to hurt others to become rich. He also doesn't want you to treat others badly if you have more than they do.

Write out 22:1 and 2.

_____

_____

Why do you think having a good name (known for being a godly person) is more important than having riches?

_____

_____

Morsels of Prayer

God, I know You don't hate people because they are rich. But I also know that You want all of your children to follow Your ways, be kind to others and live godly lives. I will follow Your ways all my life. I will use whatever riches You allow me to have for Your glory. Amen.

Feast on the Word

Read **Proverbs 18:13-24.**

What I learned: _____

_____

_____

My favorite verse: _____

Wealth

Morsel to Remember

Better a poor man whose walk is blameless than a fool whose lips are perverse.

Proverbs 19:1

Morsels of Wisdom

Proverbs 3:9-10 — Honor the Lord with your wealth, with the firstfruits of all your crops; then your barns will be filled to overflowing, and your vats will brim over with new wine.

Proverbs 8:18 — With me [wisdom] are riches and honor, enduring wealth and prosperity.

Proverbs 11:4 — Wealth is worthless in the day of wrath, but righteousness delivers from death.

Proverbs 11:16 — A kindhearted woman gains respect, but ruthless men gain only wealth.

Morsels of Reflection

Read 3:9-10 again. If you honor God with what you have, you will receive more. But in **11:4** we are warned not to trust in our wealth. We need to trust in God, and He will reward us with all we will ever need or want for. Write out **11:16.**

_____

_____

List some ways you can put this verse in your own life today.

_____

_____

Explain verse **8:18.**

_____

_____

What do we gain with wisdom?

_____

_____

Morsels of Prayer

Lord, I know You will give me all I ever need, plus much more.
I know I don't need to trust in riches, but only in You. Thank
You. I love You. Amen.

Feast on the Word

Read **Proverbs 19:1-14.**

What I learned: _____

_____

_____

My favorite verse: _____

Laziness

Morsel to Remember

Laziness brings on deep sleep, and the shiftless man goes hungry.

Proverbs 19:15

Morsels of Wisdom

Proverbs 10:4-5 — Lazy hands make a man poor, but diligent hands bring wealth. He who gathers crops in summer is a wise son, but he who sleeps during harvest is a disgraceful son.

Proverbs 12:27 — The lazy man does not roast his game.

Proverbs 18:9 — One who is slack in his work is brother to one who destroys.

Proverbs 20:13 — Do not love sleep or you will grow poor; stay awake and you will have food to spare.

Morsels of Reflection

Laziness is something God doesn't like. It is easy to become lazy. If you rely on someone else to help when you haven't worked as you should, then you can become lazy.

Read 10:4-5 again. What happens when a person doesn't work?

_____

_____

12:27 means a man is too lazy to even fix the food he has. He will surely starve.

In **18:9**, a lazy man is related to a man who

_____

Read 20:13 again. Does God want you to stay awake all the time? What does this verse mean in your own words?

_____

_____

On a separate sheet of paper, write a news story about a person who is too lazy to do anything for himself. Make it a funny story.

Morsels of Prayer

I get lazy sometimes, Lord. I don't do the chores that are expected of me, and my room gets really messy. Help me to realize that habits I form now will affect how I am when I get older. Amen.

Feast on the Word

Read **Proverbs 19:15-29.**

What I learned: _____

_____

_____

My favorite verse: _____

The Sluggard

Morsel to Remember

Even a child is known by his actions, by whether his conduct is pure and right.

Proverbs 20:11

Morsels of Wisdom

Proverbs 6:6-8 — Go to the ant, you sluggard; consider its ways and be wise! It has no commander, no overseer or ruler, yet it stores its provisions in summer and gathers its food at harvest.

Proverbs 13:4 — The sluggard craves and gets nothing, but the desires of the diligent are fully satisfied.

Proverbs 20:4 — A sluggard does not plow in season; so at harvest time he looks but finds nothing.

Morsels of Reflection

Read 6:6-8 again. What can you learn from the ant?

_____

_____

Read 13:4 and **20:4 again.** Why does a sluggard have nothing?

_____

_____

What advice would you give the sluggard?

_____

_____

Use the Scripture to write a definition of a sluggard.

_____

_____

Morsels of Prayer

Dear Lord, I thank You that I am able to do some things for myself. Help me to always have the desire to work and earn my way. No matter what my situation in life, there is always something I can do to not be a sluggard. Amen.

Feast on the Word

Read **Proverbs 20:1-15.**

What I learned: _____

_____

_____

My favorite verse: _____

Adultery Against God

Morsel to Remember

Do not say, "I'll pay you back for this wrong!" Wait for the Lord, and he will deliver you.

Proverbs 20:22

Morsels of Wisdom

Proverbs 2:16 — It [wisdom] will save you also from the adulteress.

Proverbs 5:3-6 — For the lips of an adulteress drip honey, and her speech is smoother than oil; but in the end she is bitter as gall, sharp as a double-edged sword. Her feet go down to death; her steps lead straight to the grave. She gives no thought to the way of life; her paths are crooked, but she knows it not.

Proverbs 7:4-5 — Say to wisdom, "You are my sister," and call understanding your kinsman; they will keep you from the adulteress.

Proverbs 22:14 — The mouth of an adulteress is a deep pit; he who is under the Lord's wrath will fall into it.

Morsels of Reflection

Adultery means being unfaithful to a husband or wife. But many Scriptures in the Bible symbolize adultery as being unfaithful to God. Of course, the way to be unfaithful to God is to get involved with sin. Read the Scriptures, putting the word sin in place of adulteress. What can keep you away from sin?

_____

_____

Write a proverb to tell a friend how to stay away from sin.

_____

_____

Morsels of Prayer

I don't want to fall into sin, God. I will follow Your ways only, and live only for You. The ways of a sinner are not for me. Thank You for Your care of me. Amen.

Feast on the Word

Read **Proverbs 20:16-31.**

What I learned: _____

_____

_____

My favorite verse: _____

Honor and Disgrace

Disgrace

Morsel to Remember

To do what is right and just is more acceptable to the Lord than sacrifice.
Proverbs 21:3

Morsels of Wisdom

Proverbs 11:2 — When pride comes, then comes disgrace.

Proverbs 13:5 — The righteous hate what is false, but the wicked bring shame and disgrace.

Proverbs 14:34 — Righteousness exalts a nation, but sin is a disgrace to any people.

Proverbs 18:3 — When wickedness comes, so does contempt, and with shame comes disgrace.

Proverbs 19:26 — He who robs his father and drives out his mother is a son who brings shame and disgrace.

Morsels of Reflection

Have you ever been really ashamed of something you did? Did you ever do something that caused your parents to be really disappointed in you? Write about one of those times.

_____

_____

Read 13:5 and 18:3 again. God doesn't want you to hide in shame all of your life because you did something wrong. But He wants you to not fall into the habit of sin. That is when you are disgraced. **Read 11:2 again**. How can pride cause disgrace?

_____

_____

Does **14:34** apply to our world today? How?

_____

_____

Read 19:26. In what way could you "rob" or "drive out" a parent? List some ways.

_____

_____

Morsels of Prayer

Father, I don't want to disgrace myself or my family. Help me to follow Your ways and be righteous. Your wisdom will help me follow You all the days of my life. Amen.

Feast on the Word

Read **Proverbs 21:1-15.**

What I learned: _____

_____

_____

My favorite verse: _____

Disgraceful

Morsel to Remember

A man who strays from the path of understanding comes to rest in the company of the dead.

Proverbs 21:16

Morsels of Wisdom

Proverbs 10:5 — He who sleeps during harvest is a disgraceful son.

Proverbs 12:4 — A wife of noble character is her husband's crown, but a disgraceful wife is like decay in his bones.

Proverbs 17:2 — A wise servant will rule over a disgraceful son, and will share the inheritance as one of the brothers.

Morsels of Reflection

Read all of the verses above again. List the different people who are disgraceful.

_____

_____

Write some proverbs to tell how these people can be disgraceful also:

A bossy friend

_____

_____

A dishonest businessman

_____

_____

A student who cheats

_____

_____

A disrespectful child

_____

_____

Morsels of Prayer

Father, I know a disgraceful person is one who won't follow
Your commands. I will study Your Word and learn Your ways,
so I will not be disgraceful. Amen.

Feast on the Word

Read **Proverbs 21:16-31.**

What I learned: _____

_____

_____

My favorite verse: _____

Honor

Morsel to Remember

He who loves a pure heart and whose speech is gracious will have the king for his friend.

Proverbs 22:11

Morsels of Wisdom

Proverbs 3:35 — The wise inherit honor, but fools he holds up to shame.

Proverbs 13:18 — He who ignores discipline comes to poverty and shame, but whoever heeds correction is honored.

Proverbs 18:12 — Before his downfall a man's heart is proud, but humility comes before honor.

Proverbs 20:3 — It is to a man's honor to avoid strife, but every fool is quick to quarrel.

Proverbs 29:23 — A man's pride brings him low, but a man of lowly spirit gains honor.

Morsels of Reflection

In **3:35,** what does the wise get?

_____

_____

What happens to fools?

_____

_____

In **13:18,** who gets the honor?

_____

_____

Read 18:12. again Write out the part about humility.
(Remember that humility is the opposite of pride.)

_____

_____

Read 29:23. A lowly spirit is the same as a humble person. Who
is the most humble person you know? What makes them that
way?

_____

_____

Write out verse **20:3.** Write about a situation in which you
avoided strife or a quarrel.

_____

_____

_____

Morsels of Prayer

God, I want to be honorable. I want people to know by being
around me that I am a child of God. Help me to do the very
best that I can every day. Amen.

Feast on the Word

Read **Proverbs 22:1-15.**

What I learned: _____

_____

_____

My favorite verse: _____

Honor God and His Word

Morsel to Remember

Pay attention and listen to the sayings of the wise; apply your heart to what I teach, for it is pleasing when you keep them in your heart and have all of them ready on your lips. So that your trust may be in the Lord, I teach you today, even you.

Proverbs 22:17-19

Morsels of Wisdom

Proverbs 3:9 — Honor the Lord.

Proverbs 7:1-3 — My son, keep my words and store up my commands within you. Keep my commands and you will live; guard my teachings as the apple of your eye. Bind them on your fingers; write them on the tablet of your heart.

Proverbs 30:5-6 — Every word of God is flawless; he is a shield to those who take refuge in him. Do not add to his words.

Morsels of Reflection

Read 3:9 again. What is the best way you can honor God?

_____

_____

Read 7:1-3 again. What should you do with God's Word?

_____

_____

Write out 30:5-6.

_____

_____

_____

Write a song to honor God.

_____

_____

_____

Morsels of Prayer

You are awesome and incredible, God! I love You and I love Your Word. Thank You for giving me Your Word to have as my very own. Amen.

Feast on the Word

Read **Proverbs 22:16-29.**

What I learned: _____

_____

_____

My favorite verse: _____

My Words

Mouth

Morsel to Remember

Apply your heart to instruction and your ears to words of knowledge.
Proverbs 23:12

Morsels of Wisdom

Proverbs 10:11 —The mouth of the righteous is a fountain of life.

Proverbs 15:28 — The mouth of the wicked gushes evil.

Proverbs 18:6-7 —A fool's lips bring him strife, and his mouth invites a beating. A fool's mouth is his undoing, and his lips are a snare to his soul.

Proverbs 19:28 — The mouth of the wicked gulps down evil.

Morsels of Reflection

Your mouth can get you into real trouble sometimes, can't it? You just can't resist saying something that isn't very nice, repeating a little gossip or using words that you shouldn't! **Read 10:11 again.** What kind of words would come out of a fountain of life?

_____

_____

The opposite of **10:11** is **15:28**. Read that verse again.

What bad things does a fool's mouth cause as told in **18:6-7**?

_____

_____

Read 19:28 again. What does the mouth of the wicked gulp?

_____

_____

How can you use your mouth for good things?

_____

_____

Morsels of Prayer

God, help me to always speak good words. I don't want to put people down or tell lies, gossip or swear. Help me to remember that You are listening to every word I say, even before I say it. Amen.

Feast on the Word

Read **Proverbs 23:1-18.**

What I learned: _____

_____

_____

My favorite verse: _____

Lying Tongue

Morsel to Remember

My son [child], give me your heart and let your eyes keep to my ways.
Proverbs 23:26

Morsels of Wisdom

Proverbs 12:17 — A truthful witness gives honest testimony, but a false witness tells lies.

Proverbs 12:19 — Truthful lips endure forever, but a lying tongue lasts only a moment.

Proverbs 19:5 — A false witness will not go unpunished, and he who pours out lies will not go free.

Proverbs 19:22 — Better to be poor than a liar.

Proverbs 26:28 — A lying tongue hates those it hurts.

Morsels of Reflection

Do you know someone who lies a lot? Can you trust this person with your secrets? Can you believe what this person says? **Read 12:17 and 12:19 again.** How long will a lying tongue last? How long do truthful lips last?

_____

_____

Read 19:5 again. What will happen to those who lie?

_____

_____

In **19:22** it is better to be _____ than a liar.

In **26:28,** who does a lying tongue hate? _____

Have you ever told a lie? Did you hate the person you told the lie to or about? Of course you didn't. But the Bible says we do.

How can you not hate or hurt those around you?

_____

_____

Morsels of Prayer

Lord, I don't mean to hurt anyone. I don't want to be a liar. Help me to control my tongue. Amen.

Feast on the Word

Read **Proverbs 23:19-35.**

What I learned: _____

_____

_____

My favorite verse: _____

My Tongue

Morsel to Remember

Fear the Lord and the king, my son [child], and do not join with the rebellious, for those two will send sudden destruction upon them, and who knows what calamities they can bring?

Proverbs 24:21-22

Morsels of Wisdom

Proverbs 10:19-20 — When words are many, sin is not absent, but he who holds his tongue is wise. The tongue of the righteous is choice silver.

Proverbs 12:18 — Reckless words pierce like a sword, but the tongue of the wise brings healing.

Proverbs 15:4 — The tongue that brings healing is a tree of life, but a deceitful tongue crushes the spirit.

Proverbs 25:15 — A gentle tongue can break a bone.

Morsels of Reflection

When has someone hurt you with sharp words? When have you hurt someone else with sharp words? Ask God to help you use good words all of the time.

Read the Scriptures again. Write the good things a tongue can do.

_____

_____

Write the bad things a tongue can cause.

_____

_____

_____

Write a letter to your tongue. Tell it to mind its manners. Use some words from the Scriptures.

_____

_____

Morsels of Prayer

Lord, I want my tongue to praise You always. I love You. Amen.

Feast on the Word

Read **Proverbs 24:1-17.**

What I learned: _____

_____

_____

My favorite verse: _____

	TO MY TONGUE

Gossip

Morsel to Remember

Do not gloat when your enemy falls; when he stumbles, do not let your heart rejoice, or the Lord will see and disapprove and turn his wrath away from him.

Proverbs 24:17-18

Morsels of Wisdom

Proverbs 11:13 — A gossip betrays a confidence, but a trustworthy man keeps a secret.

Proverbs 16:28 — A perverse man stirs up dissension, and a gossip separates close friends.

Proverbs 18:8 (and 26:22) — The words of a gossip are like choice morsels; they go down to a man's inmost parts.

Proverbs 20:19 — A gossip betrays a confidence, so avoid a man who talks too much.

Proverbs 26:20 — Without wood a fire goes out; without gossip a quarrel dies down.

Morsels of Reflection

Have you ever been hurt by gossip? Have you hurt someone with gossip? Tell about a time when gossip really hurt someone, whether it was you who gossiped or not.

_____

_____

_____

How hard is it to undo gossip?

_____

_____

Read 11:13 again. If you gossip, will your friends trust you with secrets?

_____

_____

Write what you have learned about gossip from these Scriptures.

_____

_____

Morsels of Prayer

Lord, help me not to gossip about anyone. It is easy to fall into that trap, but with Your help I will not gossip anymore. Amen.

Feast on the Word

Read **Proverbs 24:18-34.**

What I learned: _____

_____

_____

My favorite verse: _____

Slander

Morsel to Remember

Do not exalt yourself.

Proverbs 25:6

Morsels of Wisdom

Proverbs 10:18 — Whoever spreads slander is a fool.

Proverbs 30:10 — Do not slander a servant to his master, or he will curse you, and you will pay for it.

Proverbs 12:17 — A false witness tells lies.

Proverbs 14:25 — A truthful witness saves lives, but a false witness is deceitful.

Proverbs 25:18 — Like a club or a sword or a sharp arrow is the man who gives false testimony against his neighbor.

Morsels of Reflection

Has someone ever been a false witness against you?

_____

_____

Have you ever told a lie to be a false witness about someone else?

_____

_____

Read 10:18 again. Using your words this way is foolish! God does not approve!

In **12:17,** it is the same as lying. In **14:25,** it is deceitful.

Write out **25:18.**

_____

_____

Morsels of Prayer

Father, I ask Your forgiveness for the false things I have said about someone. It is not right and I am very sorry. Help me to stand strong against the temptation to slander someone. Amen.

Feast on the Word

Read **Proverbs 25:1-14.**

What I learned: _____

_____

_____

My favorite verse: _____

All Of Me

My Eyes

Morsel to Remember

If your enemy is hungry, give him food to eat; if he is thirsty, give him water to drink.

Proverbs 25:21

Morsels of Wisdom

Proverbs 20:12 — Ears that hear and eyes that see — the Lord has made them both.

Proverbs 21:4 — Haughty eyes and a proud heart, the lamp of the wicked, are sin!

Proverbs 23:26 — My son, give me your heart and let your eyes keep to my ways.

Proverbs 28:27 — He who gives to the poor will lack nothing, but he who closes his eyes to them receives many curses.

Morsels of Reflection

Read 20:12 again. What has the Lord made?

_____

_____

In **21:4,** what are sins?

_____

_____

Read 28:27 again. What does God want you to do when you see someone who is poor?

_____

_____

What happens to those who close their eyes to the poor and refuse to help?

_____

_____

Write out verse **23:26.**

_____

_____

_____

Morsels of Prayer

I will use my eyes for Your glory, Father. Always and forever! I love You. Amen.

Feast on the Word

Read **Proverbs 25:15-28.**

What I learned: _____

_____

_____

My favorite verse: _____

My Ears

Morsel to Remember

Apply your heart to instruction and your ears to words of knowledge.
Proverbs 23:12

Morsels to Remember

Proverbs 2:1-2, 5 — My son, if you accept my words and store up my commands within you, turning your ear to wisdom and applying your heart to understanding, then you will understand the fear of the Lord and find the knowledge of God.

Proverbs 18:15 — The heart of the discerning acquires knowledge; the ears of the wise seek it out.

Proverbs 21:13 — If a man shuts his ears to the cry of the poor, he too will cry out and not be answered.

Proverbs 28:9 — If anyone turns a deaf ear to the law, even his prayers are detestable.

Morsels of Reflection

Read 2:1-2, 5 again. If you listen to wisdom, what will you find?

_____

_____

In **18:15** what to the ears of the wise seek out?

_____

_____

Which verse talks about the cry of the poor?

_____

_____

What does God expect us to do?

_____

_____

In **28:9,** why would someone's prayers be detestable to God?

_____

_____

Write out the memory verse here.

_____

_____

Write a poem to God, telling Him you will hear His Word and gain wisdom.

_____

_____

Morsels of Prayer

Father I will always listen to Your Word and try to do what You want me to do. I will listen to Your commands and follow Your ways all my life. Amen.

Feast on the Word

Read **Proverbs 26:1-14.**

What I learned: _____

_____

_____

My favorite verse: _____

My Mouth

Morsel to Remember

The sluggard [lazy person] is wiser in his own eyes than seven men who answer discreetly.

Proverbs 26:16

Morsels of Wisdom

Proverbs 8:7-8 — My mouth speaks what is true, for my lips detest wickedness. All of the words of my mouth are just; none of them is crooked or perverse.

Proverbs 20:17 — Food gained by fraud tastes sweet to a man, but he ends up with a mouth full of gravel.

Proverbs 30:32 — If you have played the fool and exalted yourself, or if you have planned evil, clap your hand over your mouth!

Morsels of Reflection

Verses 8:7-8 speak of wisdom. Are all your words as those in 8:8?

_____

_____

Read the two funny verses, 20:17 and 30:32. Draw a picture below of one or both of them.

What do these two verses teach you?

_____

_____

On a separate sheet of paper, write a story about someone who was always planning evil and God made her walk around with her hand over her mouth.

Morsels of Prayer

God, help me to guard what comes out of my mouth. I don't want to be known as someone who plans evil or talks foolishly. I don't want to gain things by dishonesty. Help me to keep on the right path. Amen.

Feast on the Word

Read **Proverbs 26:15-28.**

What I learned: _____

_____

_____

My favorite verse: _____

My Feet

Morsel to Remember

Let another praise you, and not your own mouth; someone else, and not your own lips.

Proverbs 27:2

Morsels of Wisdom

Proverbs 1:15-16 — My son, do not go along with them, do not set foot on their paths; for their feet rush in sin.

Proverbs 3:21, 23 — My son, preserve sound judgment and discernment, do not let them out of your sight. Then you will go on your way in safety, and your foot will not stumble.

Proverbs 4:14 — Do not set foot on the path of the wicked or walk in the way of evil men.

Proverbs 4:26-27 — Make level paths for your feet and take only ways that are firm. Do not swerve to the right or the left; keep your foot from evil.

Morsels of Reflection

Read 1:15-16 again. We are warned not to follow sinners. Write about a time when someone tried to get you to sin.

_____

_____

Read 3:21 and 23 again. What will happen if you have sound judgment and make right choices?

_____

_____

Read 4:14 and 4:26-27 again. What kind of paths should you walk on?

_____

_____

Draw a map below of where you walked today or yesterday. Write on the map any times when sin fell in your way.

Morsels of Prayer

God, I will be more careful of where I go and what I do. It is important to guard my feet and make sure I go on the right path. Amen.

Feast on the Word

Read **Proverbs 27:1-14.**

What I learned: _____

_____

_____

My favorite verse: _____

My Hands

Morsel to Remember

As water reflects a face, so a man's heart reflects the man.

Proverbs 27:19

Morsels of Wisdom

Proverbs 6:10-11 & 24:33 — A little sleep, a little slumber, a little folding of the hands to rest — and poverty will come on you like a bandit and scarcity like an armed man.

Proverbs 10:4 — Lazy hands make a man poor, but diligent hands bring wealth.

Proverbs 12:24 — Diligent hands will rule, but laziness ends in slave labor.

Morsels of Reflection

What happens when you don't work?

_____

_____

Think about a time you got into trouble at home. Was it because you had nothing to do? Keeping busy will help keep you out of trouble. Write a list of things you can do at home to help out your parents.

_____

_____

Write a list of things you enjoy doing with your hands.

_____

_____

When you have nothing to do, try doing something from one of these lists!

Morsels of Prayer

I want to keep busy for You, God. I will think of ways to help at home and to serve You also. Amen.

Feast on the Word

Read **Proverbs 27:15-27.**

What I learned: _____

_____

_____

My favorite verse: _____

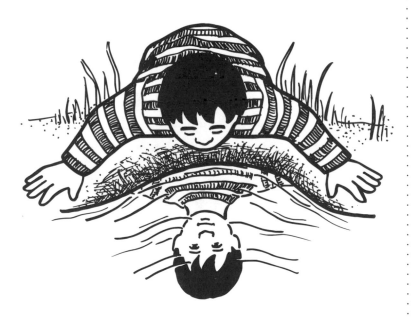

My Heart

Morsel to Remember

Evil men do not understand justice, but those who seek the Lord understand it fully.

Proverbs 28:5

Morsels of Wisdom

Proverbs 2:10 — For wisdom will enter your heart, and knowledge will be pleasant to your soul.

Proverbs 3:5 — Trust in the Lord with all your heart and lean not on your own understanding.

Proverbs 4:4 — Lay hold of my words with all your heart.

Proverbs 4:23 — Above all else, guard your heart, for it is the wellspring of life.

Proverbs 14:30 — A heart at peace gives life to the body.

Proverbs 15:13 — A happy heart makes the face cheerful, but heartache crushes the spirit.

Proverbs 15:14 — The discerning heart seeks knowledge, but the mouth of a fool feeds on folly.

Proverbs 15:15 — All the days of the oppressed are wretched, but the cheerful heart has a continual feast.

Morsels of Reflection

Read 2:10 again. What is pleasant to your soul?

_____

_____

Write out **3:5.**

_____

_____

Read 4:4 and 4:23 again. What are we to do with our hearts?

_____

_____

14:30; 15:13 and 15:15 talk about happy hearts. Tell about each verse. What does this mean to you?

_____

_____

Read 15:14 again. Which would you rather seek with your heart: knowledge or folly?

_____

_____

Morsels of Prayer

I will put Your Word in my heart, Lord, and follow You the best I can. I love You! Amen.

Feast on the Word

Read **Proverbs 28:1-13.**

What I learned: _____

_____

_____

My favorite verse: _____

My Soul

Morsel to Remember

Blessed is the man who always fears the Lord, but he who hardens his heart falls into trouble.

Proverbs 28:14

Morsels of Wisdom

Proverbs 2:10 — For wisdom will enter your heart, and knowledge will be pleasant to your soul.

Proverbs 11:30 — The fruit of the righteous is a tree of life, and he who wins souls is wise.

Proverbs 19:8 — He who gets wisdom loves his own soul.

Proverbs 22:5 — In the paths of the wicked lie thorns and snares, but he who guards his soul stays far from them.

Morsels of Reflection

Read 2:10 again. What is pleasant to the soul?

_____

_____

In **11:30,** what does a wise person do? How can you do that?

_____

_____

Write out **19:8.**

_____

_____

_____

Read 22:5 again. What do you think are thorns and snares that might be trying to trap you today? How do you stay away from them?

_____

_____

Morsels of Prayer

Father, help me to guard my soul against sin. And help me to win souls for You. I don't want anyone to miss heaven, so I will try to win as many people as I can. Amen.

Feast on the Word

Read **Proverbs 28:14-28.**

What I learned: _____

_____

_____

My favorite verse: _____

My Body

Morsel to Remember

A wise man keeps himself under control.

Proverbs 29:11

Morsels of Wisdom

Proverbs 3:7-8 — Fear the Lord and shun evil. This will bring health to your body and nourishment to your bones.

Proverbs 4:20, 22 — My son [child], pay attention to what I say; listen closely to my words. For they are life to those who find them and health to a man's whole body.

Proverbs 14:30 — A heart at peace gives life to the body, but envy rots the bones.

Morsels of Reflection

According to the Scriptures, what is good for your body?

_____

_____

How can staying away from evil, or listening to God's commands be good for your body?

_____

_____

Write out **4:22.**

_____

_____

Read 14:30 again. Why do you think envy rots the bones? How does envy make you feel?

_____

_____

Draw the outline of a person's body below. Write one of the verses inside the body.

Morsels of Prayer

Lord, I want to praise You and serve You with my whole body. Thank You for choosing me to be Your child. Amen.

Feast on the Word

Read **Proverbs 29:1-14.**

What I learned: _____

_____

_____

My favorite verse: _____

People Around Me

Friends

Morsel to Remember

Whoever trusts in the Lord is kept safe.

Proverbs 29:25

Morsels of Wisdom

Proverbs 16:28 — A perverse man stirs up dissension, and a gossip separates close friends.

Proverbs 22:24-25 — Do not make friends with a hot-tempered man, do not associate with one easily angered, or you may learn his ways and get yourself ensnared.

Proverbs 27:9 — The pleasantness of one's friend springs from his earnest counsel.

Proverbs 27:10 — Do not forsake your friend and the friend of your father.

Morsels of Reflection

Read verse 16:28 again. What does a gossip do?

_____

_____

Read 22:24-25 again. Why shouldn't you associate with someone who gets angry easily?

_____

_____

In **27:9-10,** we learn that friends help each other out. Who is your best friend? What do you love most about this friend? What can you learn about friendship from this person?

_____

_____

Morsels of Prayer

Father, I thank You for all my friends. Help me to be a good friend to others. Amen.

Feast on the Word

Read **Proverbs 29:15-27.**

What I learned: _____

_____

_____

My favorite verse: _____

Enemies

Morsel to Remember

Every word of God is flawless; he is a shield to those who take refuge in him. Do not add to his words, or he will rebuke you and prove you a liar.

Proverbs 30:5-6

Morsels of Wisdom

Proverbs 16:7 — When a man's ways are pleasing to the Lord, he makes even his enemies live at peace with him.

Proverbs 24:17 — Do not gloat when your enemy falls; when he stumbles, do not let your heart rejoice.

Proverbs 25:21 — If your enemy is hungry, give him food to eat; if he is thirsty, give him water to drink.

Morsels of Reflection

Read 16:7 again. Wouldn't it be wonderful to not have any enemies? This verse says that God will make your enemies live in peace with you, if you please God. **Read 24:17 again.** That is really hard to do, isn't it? When your enemy gets herself into trouble, you want to shout and laugh. God doesn't want you to do that. **Read 25:21** again to see how God does want you to treat your enemies. Write about someone you would like to make up with and be friends.

_____

_____

_____

_____

_____

_____

_____

Morsels of Prayer

God, I want to follow You and treat my enemies kindly. It is not always easy, but I will try to do better. Amen.

Feast on the Word

Read **Proverbs 30:1-16.**

What I learned: _____

_____

_____

My favorite verse: _____

Neighbors

Morsel to Remember

Do not plot harm against your neighbor, who lives trustfully near you.

Proverbs 3:29

Morsels of Wisdom

Proverbs 3:29-30 — Do not plot harm against your neighbor, who lives trustfully near you. Do not accuse a man for no reason — when he has done you no harm.

Proverbs 11:9 — With his mouth the godless destroys his neighbor.

Proverbs 14:21 — He who despises his neighbor sins, but blessed is he who is kind to the needy.

Proverbs 24:28-29 — Do not testify against your neighbor without cause, or use your lips to deceive. Do not say, "I'll do to him as he has done to me; I'll pay that man back for what he did."

Proverbs 25:18 — Like a club or a sword or a sharp arrow is the man who gives false testimony against his neighbor.

Proverbs 26:18-19 — Like a madman shooting firebrands or deadly arrows is a man who deceives his neighbor and says, "I was only joking!"

Morsels of Reflection

How does God want you to treat your neighbors? Write some specific things you are <u>not</u> to do to your neighbors.

_____

_____

_____

_____

Write about a good neighbor that you have. What do you like best about this person or family?

_____

_____

_____

How could you be a better neighbor?

_____

_____

Morsels of Prayer

Father, You give us specific ways to treat others. I will try to follow these things and be a good neighbor. Amen.

Feast on the Word

Read **Proverbs 30:17-33.**

What I learned: _____

_____

_____

My favorite verse: _____

Those Around Me

Family

Morsel to Remember

Speak up and judge fairly; defend the rights of the poor and needy.

Proverbs 31:9

Morsels of Wisdom

Proverbs 18:24 — A man of many companions may come to ruin, but there is a friend who sticks closer than a brother.

Proverbs 7:4 — Say to wisdom, "You are my sister."

Proverbs 15:20 — A wise son brings joy to his father, but a foolish man despises his mother.

Morsels of Reflection

In **18:24,** can you guess who that friend is?

_____

7:4 says that wisdom should be our sister. In **15:20,** we learn that wisdom makes our parents proud of us, but foolishness doesn't. How can these verses help you live better in your family?

_____

_____

_____

Write a thank you note to your whole family.

_____

_____

_____

_____

Write a thank you note to your brother, Jesus.

_____

_____

_____

Morsels of Prayer

Dear God, I thank You for my family. I also thank You for making me understand that Jesus and You and all the teachings You give me are as close to me as family. I can live better for You because of it. Thank You. Amen.

Feast on the Word

Read **Proverbs 31:1-9.**

What I learned: _____

_____

_____

My favorite verse: _____

THANK YOU NOTE

Fruit of the Spirit

Morsel to Remember

But the fruit of the Spirit is love, joy, peace, patience, kindness,
goodness, faithfulness, gentleness and self-control.

Galatians 5:22-23

Morsels of Wisdom

Look up each Scripture below and write it out. There is one for
each of the fruits of the Spirit in the memory verse above.

Love — **Proverbs 10:12**

_____

_____

Joy — **Proverbs 15:30**

_____

_____

Peace — **Proverbs 16:7**

_____

_____

Patience — **Proverbs 19:11**

_____

_____

Kindness — **Proverbs 11:17**

_____

_____

Goodness — **Proverbs 11:27**

_____

_____

Faithfulness — **Proverbs 28:20**

_____

_____

Gentleness — **Proverbs 15:1**

_____

_____

Self-control — **Proverbs 29:11**

_____

_____

Morsels of Reflection

For each of the fruits of the Spirit, think of one person you know who shows that fruit very well. Think about how you can learn from each one.

_____

_____

Morsels of Prayer

Father, I want to be this kind of person. I will work on each of the fruits listed. Thank You for Your Word. Amen.

Feast on the Word

Read **Proverbs 31:10-31.**

What I learned: _____

_____

_____

My favorite verse: _____

In Conclusion

Which proverb did I enjoy most?

_____

_____

_____

Which proverb is easiest to follow?

_____

_____

_____

Which proverb is hardest to follow?

_____

_____

_____

How do I feel about God?

_____

_____

_____

How does God feel about me?

_____

_____

_____